A PAST and PRESENT Companion

The South Devon Railway
Past and Present

Happy 4th birthday Lucas

lots of love Granny & Grandad

The South Devon Railway
Past and Present

John Brodribb

Past & Present Publishing Ltd

© John Brodribb 2012

All rights reserved. No part of this publication may be reproduced, stored in a retrieval system or transmitted, in any form or by any means, electronic, mechanical, photocopying, recording or otherwise, without prior permission in writing from Past & Present Publishing Ltd.

First published in 2012

British Library Cataloguing in Publication Data

A catalogue record for this book is available from the British Library.

ISBN 978 1 85895 279 6

Past & Present Publishing Ltd
The Trundle
Ringstead Road
Great Addington
Kettering
Northants NN14 4BW

Tel/Fax: 01536 330588
email: sales@nostalgiacollection.com
Website: www.nostalgiacollection.com

Printed and bound in the Czech Republic

Title page: **0-4-2T No 1420 heads south from Buckfastleigh with a scheduled Dart Valley service in April 1974.** *JB*

This page: **No 1420 is seen again, posing as an auto-train at Buckfastleigh in June 1978.** *JB*

Opposite: **A Dart Valley trains runs between Staverton and Buckfastleigh in May 1980, with the 'Devon Belle' observation car bringing up the rear.** *JB*

Contents

Introduction	8
Ashburton	10
Buckfastleigh	26
South from Buckfastleigh	58
Staverton	67
Napper's Crossing and Dartington	92
Totnes Littlehempston (SDR)	99
Totnes (GW main line)	110
Totnes Quay	125

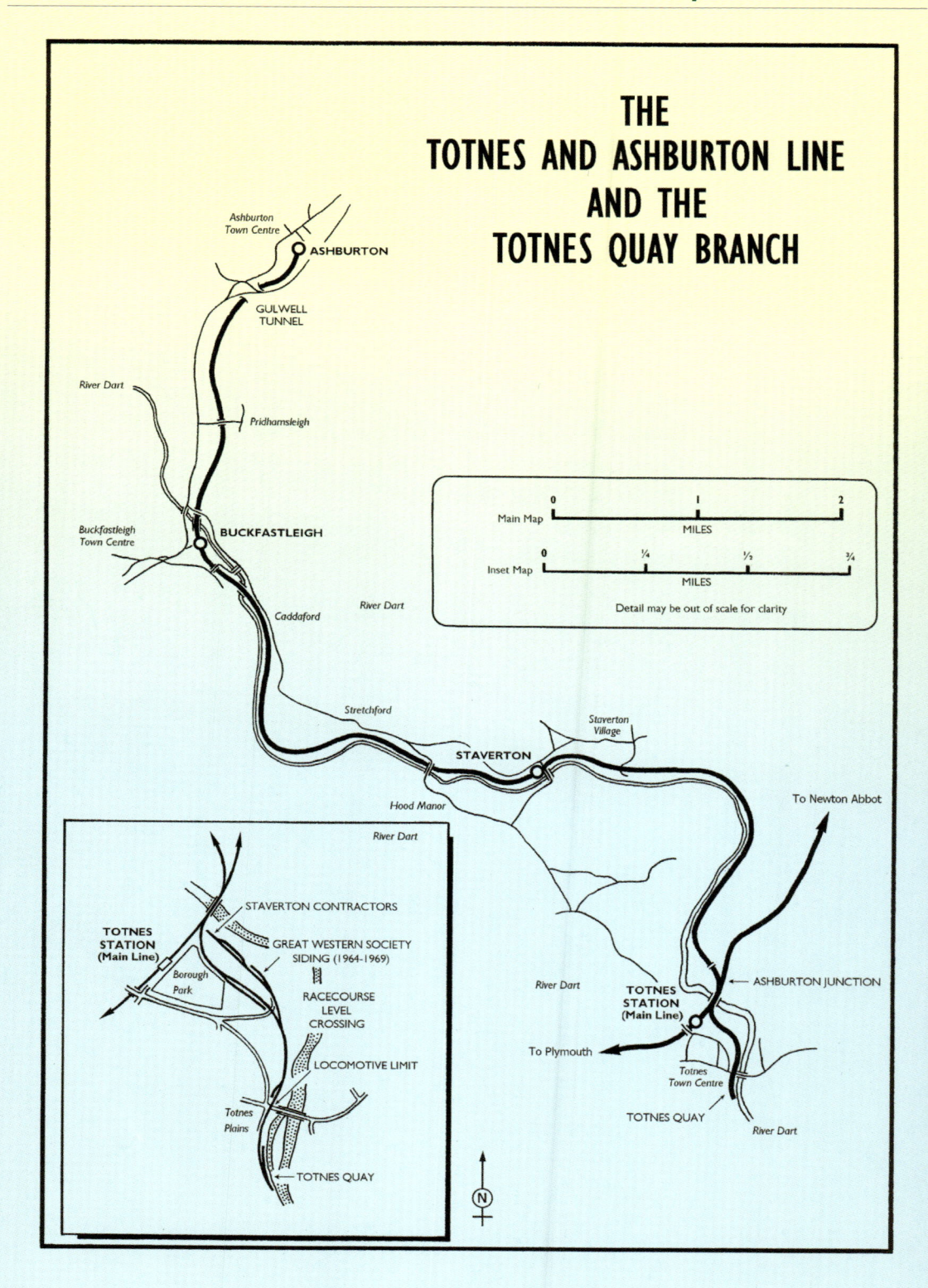

The South Devon Railway Past and Present

THE TOTNES AND ASHBURTON LINE AND THE TOTNES QUAY BRANCH

Buckfast Abbey
Town Centre
A38 Devon Expressway to Exeter and M5
A38 Devon Expressway to Plymouth
Dart Bridge Junction
BUCKFASTLEIGH STATION
PAPER MILL BRIDGE
A384
NURSERY POOL BRIDGE
Caddaford
SITE OF IRON ORE QUARRY SIDING
Stretchford
Charlies Cross
Riverford Farm
Hood Bridge - often shown on maps as Riverford Bridge
Hood Manor - now Rudolf Steiner School
BISHOP'S BRIDGE PASSING LOOP
A384
STAVERTON STATION
Huxham's Cross
Staverton Bridge (Width restricted)
Staverton Village (for Sea Trout Inn)
NAPPER'S HALT AND NAPPER'S CROSSING
Dartington
River Dart
Pumping Station
A385
A381
Woodville
Pumping Station
Totnes Rare Breeds Farm
TOTNES LITTLEHEMPSTON STATION
Totnes Station (Main Line)
FOOTBRIDGE LINK
Alan Taylor © 2007

Introduction

The present-day South Devon Railway has a surprisingly complex history, given that it was a very minor branch – possibly only a twig – of the Great Western for much of its existence. The towns of Ashburton and Buckfastleigh, on the southern edge of Dartmoor, have long been on the main road between Exeter and Plymouth, and also look towards Newton Abbot and Torquay. When the railway age started it was natural for them to want a connection with the outside world, since both had been prosperous communities with significant industries. Ashburton was a stannary town, and had other mineral workings, such as umber. Buckfastleigh was primarily a woollen town, but with paper-making also important locally. Both were also important for livestock, in different ways.

Early railway schemes envisaged linking Ashburton with Newton, which had been reached by the broad-gauge South Devon Railway as early as 1847. The line was worked by the ill-fated atmospheric system for much of 1848 before it was abandoned, although the cost meant that the main line had far more single track than it should. The Ashburton, Newton & South Devon Railway received its Act in 1846, and there had already been a rival Buckfastleigh, Totnes & South Devon Junction Railway scheme, which failed in that same year. The new scheme also failed, however, in part because the financial problems of the South Devon caused it to withdraw financial support.

In 1861 schemes were mooted under the banner of 'Devon Central Railways', and eventually this resulted in the Teign Valley line. Ashburton and Buckfastleigh interests again promoted rival schemes connecting their towns with Newton and Totnes respectively, and ultimately the latter were successful. The new Buckfastleigh, Totnes & South Devon Railway received its Act in 1864, with another in 1865 authorising extension to Ashburton. The general state of the economy imposed severe delays, and it was not until early 1870 that work resumed in earnest. The line finally opened to the public on 1 May 1872, with the usual processions, feasts and other celebrations in both Buckfastleigh and Ashburton. Work on the Totnes Quay branch had been deliberately delayed until the main line could be opened, and was itself opened in November 1873.

The Ashburton branch was laid to the South Devon Railway's broad gauge of 7ft 0¼in, with the typical baulk road of bridge rail on longitudinal timbers. It was duly narrowed over the famous weekend of 20-22 May 1892, when all the remaining broad-gauge lines west of Exeter were converted.

The train service was never frequent, and a very brief experiment with a steam railmotor in 1904-5 was followed by the Class '517' 0-4-2T and train of four-wheeled coaches, which it had itself supplanted. The Sunday service finally finished in 1917. 'Auto' working was introduced in 1927, initially also using the Class '517' tanks, and later the '48xx' Class, which many people still recall. Goods services were latterly in the hands of the '44xx' 2-6-2T locomotives, with the slightly larger '45xxs' also important. Ashburton had its own loco shed, but goods trains worked to and from Newton Abbot every day, although Laira took over at the very end of the line's existence under British Railways.

Competition from road transport – buses, lorries and cars – meant that the Ashburton branch was an early candidate for closure. Dr Richard Beeching famously said in 1969 that if he hadn't closed it then he couldn't have reopened it, but didn't mention that both passenger and goods services had been withdrawn before his *Reshaping of British Railways* report had appeared in 1963.

Early moves had been made to use the branch as a tourist attraction, so it was left largely intact after closure in 1962. The Dart Valley Light Railway Company moved onto the branch in 1965, the first signs of activity being the arrival of locomotives Nos 3205 and 4555, both then privately preserved. A supporting group for volunteers was quickly set up, the DVR Association, although the company employed paid staff almost from the outset.

Services restarted at Easter 1969, becoming only the third operational standard-gauge preserved line in Britain, after the Bluebell and the Keighley & Worth Valley. It was not possible to

Introduction

run into Totnes station, so trains were either auto-worked or topped-and-tailed until a loop was built on the Buckfastleigh side of Ashburton Junction, Totnes. Timetabled services never resumed to Ashburton, since there were plans to build the Devon Expressway, an upgraded A38, on that part of the trackbed. Even so, work was done to refurbish the station there, and the goods shed became the railway's locomotive workshop. The axe finally fell in 1971, with the last trains running to Ashburton on 2 October. Lifting of the track followed swiftly, and some items that could have been reused, such as the water tower and column, were scrapped. The orchard and fields between the railway and river at Buckfastleigh became a construction depot for the road, and the old goods yard largely disappeared beneath it. For a time locomotives had to run to and from Staverton, where there were almost no facilities – the station did not even have mains electricity at the time.

The Dart Valley Railway took over the Paignton to Kingswear line at the very end of 1972, and tended to concentrate more of its resources there because of the greater passenger potential. With numbers falling on the original line, the DVR Association ran it in 1991, with the newly formed South Devon Railway Trust taking over in 1992. The SDRT finally completed the purchase of the freehold in February 2010.

A 'Past & Present' book on this railway presents some interesting challenges. The railway has gone from Ashburton completely, although many of the station buildings remain for the time being. Most of the trackbed between there and Buckfastleigh has been obliterated by the A38, as has almost all of the original yard at Buckfastleigh. The land between the railway and river has been completely changed in terms of levels and usage. Staverton is least changed, although it now sports a permanent way yard, large signal box and passing loop. The preserved line has never had its own platform or access to Totnes station, so everything that the Dart Valley and South Devon have put on the site at Littlehempston is new. However, the connection with the main line remains, and sees occasional use.

The line has now reached its 140th anniversary, and is one of Devon's most popular attractions. Many of its volunteers started way back in the 1960s when standard-gauge railway preservation was in its infancy, but it is encouraging that there are many people involved today who cannot possibly remember the Dart Valley ever running the line.

What was lost: a view of Ashburton station in 1968. By this time the goods shed was performing the function of a locomotive repair workshop. *JB*

Ashburton

The Buckfastleigh, Totnes & South Devon Railway officially opened for business on 1 May 1872. As outlined in the Introduction, many earlier schemes had been promoted to join both Ashburton and Buckfastleigh to the South Devon's main line and, despite the name of the local company, circumstances forced it to pay careful attention to Ashburton; in the end, the citizens of the town provided a considerable amount of the money needed for its construction. The line's engineer was P. J. Margary, who had the same post with the South Devon Railway, so it is no surprise that Ashburton station (and others on the branch) had similarities to other SDR stations, notably Exeter St Thomas and Moretonhampstead. The wooden train shed covered both the passenger platform and livestock pens, with the goods shed also adjacent to the platform. Because passenger services were auto-worked there was no need to run round, so the whole train – engine and one coach – would go over to the water column. A spare trailer was kept for when strengthening was needed, such as on the school train.

The first photo shows Newton Abbot's 0-4-2T No 1427 with a single trailer, after auto-working had finished in 1957; the spare coach can be seen alongside.
   The second view shows the station in July 1968, in early Dart Valley days, with one of the friction-drive Wickham trolleys on an inspection visit by Inspector Ashley Burgess.
   By March 2012 the railway was but a distant memory, with the track long gone and buildings and land put to other uses. The recently refurbished goods shed houses a firm of architects, while the train shed and main station buildings form part of the Chuley Road garage. *Peter Gray/JB (2)*

Ashburton

This is the station and train shed at Ashburton, looking from St Lawrence Lane. In railway days the site was enclosed by steel spear fencing, with the biggest crowds being on cattle fair days, both people and livestock. The main station buildings were on the west side, including booking office, porters' room and oil store. Passengers entered through the booking office, and there was another exit at the Buckfastleigh end of the train shed. After British Railways closed the line to passengers in 1958 there were no more scheduled services, although some special trains ran in heritage days. The most notable of these were on the very last day, 2 October 1971 – Ashburton just failed to reach its centenary.

The view below shows the station in 1968 after refurbishment work by the Dart Valley Railway, including the hanging signs on the platform. Unusually for the GWR they were enamel, with blue letters on a white background and came from Tiverton station.

The station was used for storage of rolling stock before final closure, and the picture on the right features the 0-4-0ST Peckett locomotive from Exeter Gas Works, which had arrived in 1969. Various engineering wagons are stabled to the left. *Both JB*

The final day was probably one of the busiest in the line's history. In the first picture (right) the first train of the final day has arrived, a through working of Dart Valley stock from Totnes BR, hauled by 2-6-2T No 4588, with the 'Devon Belle' observation car at the other end.

Later in the day (above) the very last passenger train to arrive at the terminus was headed by two 0-6-0 pannier tanks, Nos 6435 (leading) and 1638. It had originated at Paddington, and may have been unique in running non-stop through Buckfastleigh.

Today the train shed and station buildings are occupied by Station Garage, although this may not be for much longer. The area between the platforms has been filled in, and many of the timber stanchions clearly seen in the picture on the previous page have been removed and replaced by steel, with a lean-to extension built out to the road boundary. Plans are in hand for the complete redevelopment of the site. *JB (2)/Sarah Anne Harvey*

Ashburton

The cattle pens can clearly be seen as No 1427 goes on shed – probably to take water – on 25 October 1958. It appears to be taking the coach with it, a practice continued from the days of auto-working. St Lawrence's church is in the background, while the pad for dealing with animal effluent can clearly be seen.

In the second picture 2-6-2T No 4555 is about to be coaled in 1970. Today the old train shed is wider than before, has been reclad and has had a lean-to added across the end of the building. The well where the track once ran has been filled in, and the motor car reigns supreme.
Peter Gray/Robin Leach/JB

Ashburton was provided with both a water tank and a water column, adjacent to Chuley Road. It was the usual practice for the loco to remain coupled to its auto-coach when going across to take water, since the uncoupling and recoupling of the auto-gear, as well as the other normal connections between the two, would have been onerous and time-consuming – and the timetable was not exactly tight. Even after auto-working ceased, the practice seems to have continued. In Dart Valley days passenger services did not work to or from Ashburton, so engines were prepared and disposed there but the passenger coaches remained at Buckfastleigh. No 1427 is seen on the shed road with its single suburban trailer, actually taking coal, some time during the summer of 1958.

In contrast, Class 03 No D2192 stands opposite the tank on 27 August 1971, only a month or so before the final closure.

Ashburton

Sadly, after the station had finally closed and the track lifted, the water tank was pulled down on top of the column and both went for scrap. The exact viewpoint for the modern photo is not possible, but the house on the hillside, now bright pink, is the same as that behind the old water tank. *Peter Gray/Robin Leach (3)/JB*

Passenger trains ran from Ashburton to Totnes with the locomotive running chimney-first at the Totnes end, although running round was necessary after auto-working finished. Signalling remained primitive until the end, and the signal box was never built. The starting signal was controlled by a single lever on the platform end, with no interlocking with anything else! The first photograph shows No 1427 leaving with an afternoon train late in 1957, the signal already having been returned to danger by the platform staff. St Lawrence's church provides the fixed point in the background, and there are covered wagons in the goods shed road. The siding in the foreground extended back to Tuckers' maltings, and when the second picture was taken in 1968 there was a ventilated van standing there. The Dart Valley Railway did not reinstate any signalling at Ashburton, and by this time the goods shed was performing the function of locomotive repair workshop.

The third view shows 0-6-0PT No 1638 standing in the loop on 27 August 1971, with the loco pit in the foreground.

Ashburton

By the time No 1420 was photographed on 2 October 1971 changes were already taking place, with materials being moved to Buckfastleigh prior to final closure. The 0-4-2T is here seen on probably the heaviest train of its career, the through working from Ashburton to Swansea, the penultimate train from the terminus.

Most of the station area has now been divided up into separate business units, separated by secure fencing. Buildings across the trackbed block viewpoints, and there is no elevated position corresponding to the water tower. The 'present' view was taken from Chuley Road and helps to illustrate the point; the fence on the left is where the railway boundary once was, and the goods shed and St Lawrence's church remain. The white building to the right of the goods shed is an extension on the end of the train shed, which still exists and is part of the garage. The road going to the left has been built since the railway went. *Peter Gray/JB/Robin Leach/Nick Givens/JB*

The water tower provided an excellent vantage point for photographs of Ashburton station, although its absence today, and that of any corresponding vantage point, make it almost impossible to get a 'present' photograph. The earlier one is probably taken from the post of the starting signal. In both views – one from early days, probably Great Western, and the other from the 1970 Dart Valley era – there are a number of common points to aid identification. As ever, the church tower can be seen, and both show the gas holder in the right background. In the earlier view the goods shed still has its original lean-to office, which was replaced around 1950 by the brick structure seen in the later view. The old coach body, once to the left of the locomotive standing outside the goods shed, was removed by the Dart Valley, having been used as a store by Levers. Livestock pens are obvious in the earlier view, but hidden by the tall tree in the later. *Totnes Image Bank/JB*

Ashburton

The train shed at Ashburton showed obvious affinity with other similar structures elsewhere on the original South Devon Railway. The platform line and loop terminated in buffer stops, with St Lawrence Lane and Chuley Road forming the boundaries of the station on the north and east sides. The station buildings were reached past the Locomotive inn, now the Silent Whistle, with access to the platform via the booking office. The first these photographs shows the last train, from Paddington, having arrived on 2 October 1971, and the normally shy and retiring fireman Colin Harmes signing autographs.

The second picture was taken from the passenger platform looking towards the stops. Newly arrived No 7827 *Lydham Manor* stands on the loop headshunt road awaiting restoration. The locomotive had been bought following an appeal to DVR Association members for funds, and would have been useable on the line without too much civil engineering work to strengthen bridges.

Today the building is used as a garage and the space where the tracks ran has long been filled in, although the platform can still clearly be seen. The roof is supported by an internal framework of steel girders, with most of the old wooden stanchions having been replaced by steel along the road side, and the shed extended. Both modern photos are looking northwards towards the buffer stops, with the station buildings on the left. One link with the past that is not easily visible is the old lamp room, still in use as an oil store. *Robin Leach/Ken Plowman/JB/Sarah Anne Harvey*

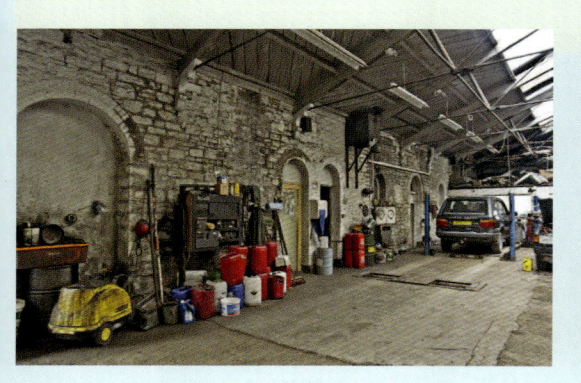

The goods shed at Ashburton was never enlarged, unlike the one at Buckfastleigh – traffic did not warrant it. The main picture shows its position alongside the passenger platform. It originally had a much larger lean-to office at the Buckfastleigh end, but this was replaced about 1950 by the red-brick structure visible to the left of the main doors. Lever's store, the old coach body, can also be seen in this 1968 view.

Conversion to workshop use is evident in the picture on the left, with Nos 6435 and 4555 standing outside.

Ashburton

Its current appearance is shown in the final two photographs, the first taken from the road side, while the other illustrates how much has gone of the track layout; there is no trace of the platform, and the track doors have been replaced by a large window. The building has recently been extensively refurbished, including reroofing. *JB/Robin Leach/Sarah Anne Harvey/JB*

The South Devon Railway Past and Present

Ashburton

When the Ashburton branch was built there was a bridge over the line very near milepost 9, just outside Ashburton. In the 1930s the town was bypassed, with the new road, now the A38, passing to the east. This necessitated a new crossing of the branch line on the site of the old bridge, and this became Gulwell Tunnel. The picture opposite shows 0-4-2T No 1420 in Dart Valley days heading for Buckfastleigh to take up its day's passenger duties; the portal of Gulwell Tunnel can be seen in front of the engine.

In earlier days, 0-4-2T No 1470, with its single coach, leaves Ashburton on 27 September 1958.

When the Ashburton bypass was dualled in the 1970s it was linked to a new road built on the alignment of the former branch. The slip roads were realigned in this area, and crossed the branch to the south of the tunnel, which was abandoned together with the road that had formerly passed over it. Today it is used as a footpath, part of Bulliver Way. The third photograph shows the approximate position of the southern portal, while the fourth is looking more or less along the trackbed immediately to the south, towards **Buckfastleigh.** *Ken Plowman/Peter Gray/ Sarah Anne Harvey (2)*

Continuing southward, the branch passed Pridhamsleigh. The first two views again show No 1420 passing a lineside garden on its way to Buckfastleigh, although in the latter it is probably going back to the shed after the day's work. The third photograph is very close by. *All Ken Plowman*

Ashburton

No 1466 heads for Ashburton on 16 August 1958, with the quarry buildings just visible in the background. The second view shows No 1420 starting the work of clearing stock from Ashburton prior to closure, as it takes a tool van to Buckfastleigh.

In complete contrast, the view from the bridge over the A38 shows today's scene. The road follows the alignment of the railway, and the bridge is on the site of an older one over the line. *Peter Gray/Robin Leach/Sarah Anne Harvey*

Buckfastleigh

The Ashburton branch reached Buckfastleigh by following the valley of the River Ashburn, or Yeo, a tributary of the River Dart. At the north end the line passed under the Totnes Road by means of a stone arch bridge, of which there were many on the line, then almost immediately crossed the Dart by an iron girder bridge with two stone piers, similar to but smaller than the one that survives at Nursery Pool. On the south side, between the river and railway, was the Salmon's Leap, latterly used as a café and restaurant, and which later burned down; the Mogul's Palace Indian restaurant now stands on the site. The Totnes Road bridge was much used as a vantage point for photographs, but was not pictured much itself.

The first picture illustrates the point, as the 10.30 Saturdays-only train from Totnes is hauled over the river by 0-4-2T No 1427 on 11 October 1958, with the photographer on the road bridge. The bracket signals controlled access to the loop and main platform for up trains, with the down advance starter right by the bridge. Several box vans are in the headshunt behind the train.

The second photograph is from a similar vantage point, but on the river side of the road bridge, and shows the returning special working from Ashburton to Swansea on the last day of services, headed by No 1420. *Peter Gray/Bernard Mills*

Buckfastleigh

Here is a completely different viewpoint of the river bridge, this time from river level with the Salmon's Leap in the background. It shows the last train, the special from Paddington, heading over the river and about to pass under the Totnes Road. In contrast, the second view also shows a train on the river bridge, but from an elevated viewpoint, with the Dart Bridge, then carrying the A38 over the river, the thatched Salmon's Leap ahead of the train, and the Black Rock guest house, now the Abbey Inn, in the background.

The corresponding 'present' photos are difficult, because of the A38. However, this one is from almost the same viewpoint as the first picture, although there are no obvious common reference points. The railway bridge crossed the river just in front of the large tree on the far bank of the Dart, and the white building behind the tree, the Mogul's Palace, is on the site of the old Salmon's Leap. The piers of the Dart Bridge can just about be seen through the railway bridge, but are now notable in its absence. The Ashburn is seen emptying into the Dart; it crossed under the railway just to the north of the Totnes Road bridge. *Nick Givens/Robin Leach/JB*

The Totnes Road bridge carried the A384 over the line. The first picture shows No 4555 shunting an auto-coach in the early spring of 1967, with the river bridge behind the buffer stops of the down-side headshunt, and the road bridge behind. Beyond the bridge was the only section of favourable gradient for down trains on their journey to Ashburton.

The second photograph shows the bridge after the track had been lifted and construction had started on the new A38; the parapet has also been removed and replaced by a wooden fence. The river bridge and trackbed were used by construction vehicles between their depot at Buckfastleigh – where the workshops now stand – and the construction site along the valley.

Again, it is almost impossible to obtain the matching 'present' photograph – both the A38 and the very considerable growth of trees make it difficult. The winter view of the bridge carrying the Devon Expressway across the Dart would once have shown the railway bridge in the background, and the Totnes Road curving over the line, then joining the old A38 right by the Dart Bridge. *Peter Gray/Robin Leach/JB*

Buckfastleigh

Buckfastleigh station itself was east of the town, with the railway crossing the river twice to get as close as possible. These two early views show it from the hillside above; the first dates from around 1908 or slightly later, as the goods shed extension has been built. The station building was extended slightly earlier. The station master's house is also clear, as is the Co-op's coal shed, then painted white, but black in later days; it stood where coaches now park. An exact current view would be very difficult, because of the A38 embankment and thick tree growth on it. *Both Totnes Image Bank*

The first two pictures show what happened in later years. While the railway was closed the station building was let to Calidec, an underfloor heating company. The Dart Valley used a shed next to the side entrance to the platform, and there sold day tickets for access to the site. By the time the official opening came around, in May 1969, they had taken possession of the building, and Dr Richard Beeching performed the official opening ceremony. His speech included the immortal words, 'If I hadn't closed this line I would not now be able to reopen it' – what a shame that it had actually closed to both passengers and goods before his *Reshaping of British Railways* report appeared in 1963…

Buckfastleigh

Today the appearance has been improved by a lot of care and maintenance, not least the use of what are generally reckoned to be authentic Great Western colours for the paintwork. Here is the station building in winter sunshine during February half term, when the South Devon runs auto-trains. The join between the original building and the 1906 extension can still be seen very clearly.

A school party are shortly to be 'evacuated' to the safety of rural Buckfastleigh, so a military ambulance has arrived, together with a despatch rider's bike; there is also a selection of fairly gruesome items from the ambulance that can be used to treat field injuries should there be an air raid.

Despite appearances, the goods shed has not been too much modified, although the formerly open sides have long been filled in and the 1908 extension turned into part of the South Devon's museum. *All JB*

Passengers and other users reached Buckfastleigh station along the approach road, off Station Road. The station was a fairly inconvenient distance from the town and the mills that were its main source of goods traffic, although less than the mile that often seems to be obligatory for country stations. These panoramic views show the relationship of the station to the town and surrounding countryside. The first was taken in 1970, before construction of the A38 had started. The old approach road can be seen, with four parked coaches and the station in the foreground. Look for the station master's house, now Saunders House, and the goods shed, as well as the houses on the hill behind in Dartbridge Road.

The second was taken in 1973 after construction had started. The A38 embankment can be seen, together with the newly built approach road, still in use today. Trees near the station have been cleared, so the buildings are much clearer. Look also for the piers that will carry the road to the west of Buckfastleigh, over the Old Totnes Road.

By 2012 the scenery has recovered from the scars of road building, and many more trees have grown – Saunders House can no longer be seen from this viewpoint. However, the goods shed and station building remain clear, the A38 sits on its piers, and the houses remain in Dartbridge Road. *Robin Leach (2)/IJB*

Buckfastleigh

In its final incarnation Buckfastleigh yard had quite a lot of capacity, having been enlarged to take account of its considerable traffic. Wool, paper and coal were the staples, the first two largely handled in the goods shed, and the latter in the yard. The Co-op also had a coal shed. The layout was controlled by a brick-built signal box at the Ashburton end, shortly to be reopened as part of the museum.

The first picture shows No 4555 and an auto-coach beside the box in February 1968, while No 1420 has arrived from Totnes on 23 August 1971. Its train is not auto-worked, the leading coach being one of the line's two Collett excursion Open 3rds. There was no loop at Totnes at this early stage, so trains longer than the maximum permitted four auto-coaches had to be topped and tailed.

Most of the old goods yard disappeared under the new A38, although the ends of two of the sidings remain. The main line and loop had to be severely truncated, and curved sharply to stay clear of the new earthworks. Fortunately the original signal box survived, and remained connected to the surviving points and signals for a while, before an errant bulldozer put paid to the rodding run. The third view shows how the layout has been adapted. *JB/John Leach/JB*

The South Devon Railway Past and Present

The goods shed road now joins the main line in front of the box rather than running behind, and may have to be severed completely if the platform were extended. What is now known as the 'PLOG' shed road (Private Locomotive Owners Group) also reaches the main running road via a tightly curved connection, across which the access road for the workshops now runs.
Both Sarah Anne Harvey

Buckfastleigh

The two black and white pictures show the goods yard in early Dart Valley days. The first is taken from the loading dock on the west side of the yard, now completely vanished under the café. Look for the signal box as a reference point – at this stage the yard was still in use by the Co-op for its coal business. The second picture shows the dock nearer the goods shed, with 0-4-2T No 1420 standing over a relatively new ash pit.

The 'present' view shows the remaining loading dock, now home to 0-4-0ST *Lady Angela* and other items of rolling stock, which have to be shunted through the PLOG shed. The signal box is just about visible behind the departing DMU power car. *Dave Ellis (2)/JB*

The first of these three views shows the situation earlier, nearer the signal box – note that the goods shed siding, where the coaches are standing, passes behind the signal box.

By the time the second photograph was taken in 1973 the A38 embankment is well under way, the old sidings have mostly gone, and the goods shed siding now runs in front of the box.

Things look very different today. The **PLOG** shed stands over part of the loading bank seen on the previous page, so this is the nearest one can get to take the photo. A concrete pad is home to a series of sheds housing (among others) a second-hand bookshop, the Devon Diesel Society, carriage and wagon spares and permanent way items. The signal box, which retains its original frame and locking, is being restored as part of the museum. *All JB*

Buckfastleigh

At the other end of the yard, a corner of the goods shed can be seen on the left of the photograph taken in August 1971, with the loading dock most obviously occupied by a Super Saloon. Nos 1420 and 1369 are in the right foreground. The open area is that now occupied by the containers and sheds shown on the previous page.

The second view is looking in the opposite direction, down the slope on an open day, with the Super Saloon (*Duchess of York*) on the left, and the goods shed offices on the right.

Today's view is taken from much the same viewpoint as the first, although a little further back so that the signal box is in view. In 1971 the photographer would have been standing on the track of the goods shed siding. Today the only track remaining is the realigned No 2 siding, now going via the PLOG shed to the loading dock. *Robin Leach/Dave Ellis/JB*

These 'past' viewpoints are largely impossible today because of the A38. In the first No 1420 is shunting the yard, the photographer standing on No 2 siding, and the locomotive on No 3. The Salmon's Leap and Totnes Road bridge are just visible in the background. To take the equivalent picture today you would need a very tall periscope protruding up through the central reservation of the road!

The second photograph shows a returning Sunday School excursion on 29 June 1960, in the charge of Nos 4555 and 4561. The cattle wagons in No 2 siding are very much a thing of the past. The third view shows the same train from a different angle, and includes a set of weigh scales for the coal yard.

This is as near as it is possible to get to the same viewpoint today, and even so it has been necessary to climb a little way up the bank of the road. *Dave Ellis/Peter Gray (2)/IJB*

Buckfastleigh

39

The South Devon Railway Past and Present

At the south end of the station the only track, the set of points connecting the loop and main together with the catch point in the loop. As c. seen, the Dart Valley reinstated the signalling, it looks as though permanent way work might complicating matters in the first photograph (picture). Both this and the second view *(above)* services in the height of the summer of 1969, when the lack of a loop at Totnes necessitated having a loco at each end of the train. 0-6-0PT No 6435 is taking water from one of the standpipes in the 'six foot' (the space between adjacent tracks, normally about that distance). The branch was once broad gauge, and retains the greater spacing between tracks at Buckfastleigh.

Buckfastleigh

The third picture shows 0-4-2T No 1420 at the head of a through train, with the front of the leading coach over the car park bridge. This once accommodated the lane leading down from Kilbury Mill, along which carts trundled with loads of wood pulp or finished paper. *JB (2)/Nick Givens*

The South Devon Railway Past and Present

The original signal box was ideally placed to operate the layout at Buckfastleigh. It commanded a view of the yard, and of trains arriving at and departing from the station. The first two pictures show the view from the steps in 1968 looking up the line, before it reopened. The conifer trees at the back of the loop platform feature prominently, and the second photograph also shows the old cider orchard and the land sloping gently down to the river. The railway had never owned the land beyond the loop boundary fence.

By the time the third picture was taken in 1973 much had changed. No 1420 is still shunting in the loop, but most of the old track has gone, together with the orchard and the tall trees. In its place came the new yard, formed from spoil dumped from A38 construction.

The 2011 view from the signal box steps shows the realigned goods shed siding now leading into the Carriage & Wagon shop and museum. Refurbished goods vans are headed by unrefurbished 4-6-0 No 4920 *Dumbleton Hall*, although the siding is not currently connected. Permanent way materials, including spare rails, are due for relocation to Staverton. Any extension of the passenger platform here would mean permanent severance of the goods shed siding. *JB (2)/Robin Leach/JB*

In the early days of the Dart Valley it was relatively easy to restore the appearance of a country branch line. It had been left more or less intact by British Railways, and not much more than replacement of a few signal arms and a swift paint job was needed. The permanent way volunteers might have argued about a few trees growing up through the track, and one stretch did get nicknamed 'Vietnam' because of the luxuriance of the vegetation – it does rain occasionally in South Devon. Some pleasant scenes could be recreated, though, and the first picture shows one such. 0-6-0PT No 6435 is sandwiched between four auto-coaches in the centre of the platform at Buckfastleigh, probably around 1970 when this was the normal train formation.

Buckfastleigh

The second also shows the station, this time looking at the loop from the main platform, when there were two Pullman cars on site, *Ibis* and *Car No 54*. They later went to Tyseley. Note the spruce trees in the background, identifying this as pre-Devon Expressway.

By the time the third photograph was taken in September 1977 there was an operational loop at Totnes, so the locomotive ran round at each end of its journey. However, the picture shows Nos 1450 and 1420 at each end of the Dart Valley directors' saloon. The loop platform has acquired a wall at its rear, and both locomotives have acquired names: No 1420 became *Bulliver* and No 1450 *Ashburton*.

The final picture was taken in August 1974, when everything that could steam did, for an early DVR gala. The 0-4-0ST Peckett from Exeter Gas Works, later *Ashley*, is coupled to veteran GWR 2-6-2T No 4555. *JB/Alan Rushworth/JB/Ian Holder collection*

In 1972 the Ashburton branch celebrated its centenary, although the terminus had narrowly missed out on this achievement. It was a good excuse for a special train and lots of Victorian costume, and the first photo shows the returning special with Driver Alan Gosling leaning out of the cab of No 4555. The weather looks typically Devonian.

The 'present' photo, taken from much the same viewpoint as those on the previous spread, shows auto-fitted 2-6-2T No 5526 at the head of a trial working in February 2011. The brand-new Stoneycombe ballast shows that the track has been completely relaid, probably for the first time since the old broad-gauge baulk road, with its longitudinal timbers and transoms, was replaced by more modern cross sleepers. Resignalling took place long ago, and is worked from Buckfastleigh South signal box, located by the footbridge at the south end of the station. The old signal box can be seen in the distance, and the conifers are on the A38 embankment.
Totnes Image Bank/JB

In September 2009 we see the station with no service train in view, and earlier that year No 1369 shunting the dining train into the platform to be prepared for an evening working.

Track relaying work is in progress in January 2011. The track has been removed from the platform road, and the ballast is being dug out and loaded into wagons for dumping elsewhere. New wooden sleepers are being used, to preserve the traditional appearance within station limits. *All JB*

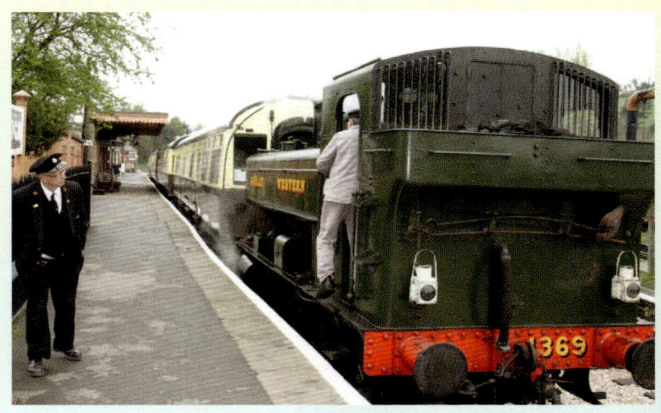

The South Devon Railway Past and Present

The Totnes end of Buckfastleigh station has long been a favourite vantage point for photographers. In the first view No 1427 heads its single coach forming the 11.17am service from Ashburton on an unspecified day towards the end of passenger services. Note the position of the station nameboard, and the fact that the platform ramp is close to the end of the corrugated-iron 'pagoda' shed. There is a camping coach in the loading dock, seen behind the nameboard.

Although the location is very similar, and the track layout still unchanged, the load for 0-4-2T No 1420 on 23 August 1971 is very different. Perhaps someone should have informed the Society for the Prevention of Cruelty to 14xxs? It is probably a Dart Valley peak-season service train, loading to seven coaches including the 'Devon Belle' observation car.

Finally we see the same scene some 40 years later, with diesel-electric No 20110 at the head of a passenger working. It is standing in exactly the same place as No 1420, but the platform has grown, and a water tower has replaced the trees on the loop platform. *Peter Gray/Robin Leach/Sarah Anne Harvey*

The extension of the platform, and the addition of the footbridge, can be seen by comparing the first two pictures, featuring No 4555 and visiting 'Dukedog' 4-4-0 No 9017. The starting signal provides a reference point.

From a similar viewpoint, but from the end of the platform, we see the recreated 40th anniversary special departing on Sunday 5 April 2009. *John Stretton/JB (2)*

Before the reopening, 2-6-2T No 4555 stands at the head of a train of coaching stock, while later 0-6-0PT No 6435 departs for Totnes with a service train.

In the third view 0-6-0PT No 1638, now at the Kent & East Sussex Railway, comes out of the new yard under the new footbridge in April 1978.

The present-day equivalent shows 0-6-0PT No 1369 at the head of the SDR dining train, in almost exactly the same position, again illustrating the point that the platform has been extended. *John Stretton/Ken Plowman/JB (2)*

Buckfastleigh

51

The footbridge at Buckfastleigh has provided a good vantage point ever since it was installed. Before that the only way to get an elevated view was to climb up a signal post. The first of these views shows the new yard from the footbridge in April 1978, with the GWR steam crane in the platform road. The new water tower, recently obtained from South Lambeth goods yard, stands at one end of the loop platform, and the new A38 is clearly shown.

The second picture was taken from the water tower – the crane has shunted into the loop, and the new running shed can be seen. The old signal box stands at the far end of the truncated layout.

The 'present' scene shows 'Dukedog' 4-4-0 No 9017 at the head of the 'Cambrian Coast Express'. *JB (2)/Steve Montgomery*

Buckfastleigh

These photographs show the view in the other direction. In April 1978 Nos 1638 and 1420 double-head a through special into Buckfastleigh, with the leading engine passing over the car park bridge. Note that the bracket signals forming the down homes are absent, having been removed by the Dart Valley Railway. They were later reinstated with an extra doll to allow direct movement into the new yard, and this can be seen in the second view. The locomotive, 0-6-0 No 3205, is in exactly the same place, and heads a brake-van special towards Staverton during 2011. *Both JB*

A typical Dart Valley auto-train leaves for Totnes during the first season of heritage operation in 1969. The locomotive is passing over what is now the car park bridge, once crossing a track from Kilbury Paper Mill to the station.

A few years later 0-4-2T No 1420 stands just beyond the bridge at the head of an excursion train returning to the main line.

Forward to April 2011, and 'Dukedog' No 9017 heads a photographers' special over the bridge. Recreating a variety of rural workings such as this milk train, the South Devon operated a complete week of special charters at the start of the locomotive's visit from the Bluebell Railway. *JB/ Nick Givens/JB*

Buckfastleigh

The first two pictures are fascinating portrayals of Buckfastleigh station, looking towards Ashburton, from or near Paper Mill bridge. The first shows that much new work has recently taken place although, as the goods shed appears not to have been extended, it predates 1908. The second view has a nearer vantage point and a later date, with Paper Mill bridge just to the right of the picture; the goods shed has been extended. The station master's house is a good reference point.

It is not possible to get an exact comparison today; photography off the bridge is blocked by housing development, as is the view from the same point as in the more distant panorama above. As a result, this photo was taken from the signal post by the bridge. Houses have been built on both sides of the cutting, and the station master's house provides the only fixed reference point. *Totnes Image Bank (2)/JB*

Paper Mill bridge takes the Old Totnes Road over the railway, and is so called because of the former Kilbury Mill on the river side, which handled goods traffic both inwards and outwards. The first two of these pictures date from the 1970s, and provide the nearest comparison to those on the previous page. The third photograph was taken from the former cart track between the mill and the station. *Ken Plowman/JB/ Ken Plowman*

Buckfastleigh

These views are looking in the opposite direction, towards Totnes. The first shows the returning Sunday School excursion on 29 June 1960, while in the second 0-6-0PT No 5786 brings a mince-pie special back from Totnes on New Year's Day 2009. *Peter Gray/JB*

South from Buckfastleigh

After passing under Paper Mill bridge and through the cutting seen on the previous page, the South Devon Railway swings round gently towards the crossing of the River Dart at Nursery Pool, passing one of the line's main scenic delights on the way – Buckfastleigh sewage works! These pictures show No 1420 passing the works with a scheduled Dart Valley service in April 1974. Among the coaches in the formation are the 'Devon Belle' observation car behind the locomotive, the Gresley buffet in the centre, and Hawksworth Brake Composite No 7377; of these, only the last is still on the line. *Both JB*

South from Buckfastleigh

These pictures show the sewage works from a slightly different viewpoint. The second shows 2-8-0 No 3803 heading a train towards Buckfastleigh on 5 April 2009, the weekend of the 40th anniversary of the reopening of the branch in the heritage era. *Both JB*

The South Devon Railway Past and Present

The line crosses the River Dart at Nursery Pool bridge. A plate girder structure with two intermediate piers in the river, it is located between the sewage works and Caddaford curve, where the branch and the main Totnes road come very close. The bridge was built to broad-gauge clearances, and when the gauge was narrowed in 1892 the track was left towards one side of the bridge, since the rail on the sewage works side was moved in towards the other. The bridge has always been a favourite spot for photographers, and the celebrated artist Terence Cuneo painted the scene for the Dart Valley Railway.

In 2004 the South Devon Railway went ahead with work to refurbish and upgrade the bridge, and the track on either side was realigned so that it could now pass over centrally. In order to preserve the appearance of the structure as much as possible a new concrete trough was constructed in the centre, bearing on the existing piers, there being enough space because of the broad gauge clearances. The track now sits in this trough, and handrails have been fitted along the length of the bridge to comply with current safety regulations.

The first photograph shows 0-4-2T No 1470 heading the 3.25pm train from Totnes on 27 September 1958, near the end of regular passenger service. Thirteen years later, on 26 August 1971, we see 2-6-2T No 4588 heading a Dart Valley train towards Totnes, with the 'Devon Belle' observation car immediately behind the locomotive. The whole bridge is almost visible in the third view, taken from the nearby Totnes road; 0-4-2T No 1420 is taking four-wheel coach W215, then in use as a mess vehicle, to Staverton prior to the start of the Easter Gala on 19 April 1976.

The other two photos (opposite) show the bridge today in both summer and winter. The first illustrates how lack of leaves on the trees can improve the view; it was taken on 1 January 2006, and shows 0-6-0PT No 5786 heading back to Buckfastleigh with the 1.00pm service from Totnes. In the other picture 2-6-2T No 5526 is in charge of an afternoon service to Buckfastleigh on 22 June 2008; the new and old parts of the structure are clearly visible in both views. *Peter Gray/Robin Leach/JB collection/JB (2)*

South from Buckfastleigh

61

Once over Nursery Pool, the railway and the A384 Totnes to Buckfastleigh road briefly become very close at Caddaford curve, with the River Dart equally close on the other side of the line. This provides and excellent vantage point for photographers, and the first two of these pictures show Dart Valley trains heading towards Staverton and Totnes, both headed by 0-6-0PT No 1638. The first was taken in August 1971, with the 'Devon Belle' as the leading vehicle. In the second – about four years later – an auto-coach is the first vehicle, and the locomotive has been through the works; its green Dart Valley livery has been replaced by British Railways black.

The South Devon Railway now has only two operational auto-coaches, but in 2010 hired in 0-4-2T No 1450, now owned by Mike Little, and his beautifully restored coach No 178. This allowed a three-car auto train to be operated for the first time for many years, seen here on Caddaford curve. The road has been realigned, and has moved even closer to the line. *Robin Leach/Ken Plowman/ Sarah Anne Harvey*

South from Buckfastleigh

Beyond Caddaford curve road and rail separate again. The road climbs up the valley side, while the branch stays much nearer the river, though largely out of sight of it. There is a long straight section that drops gently down towards Stretchford, and the vantage point from high up in the field or the roadside gives fine views of passing trains. In the first view the 4.10pm service from Ashburton to Totnes is seen on 29 March 1958 in the charge of one of Newton Abbot's '14xxs', while the second, from an almost identical viewpoint, depicts Class 31 diesel No 31149 with the Chipmans weedkiller train heading towards Buckfastleigh on 27 April 1983.

The lush growth of vegetation in the valley saw trees grow up along this stretch of line, until some prolonged attention from the SDR's volunteer cutting-back gang though the winter of 2011-12 opened up the view once more. In the first half term of 2012 2-6-2T No 5526 propels the 11.30am train from Totnes back to Buckfastleigh on 19 February, formed of auto-coaches Nos 225 and 228. *Peter Gray/Steve Montgomery/Bernard Mills*

As the line proceeds towards Staverton it first has to cross the main Totnes road again, this time passing under it at Hood Bridge. Ordnance Survey maps have identified this as Riverford Bridge for many years, but it has always been the former on the railway, and to most local people. The railway is very close to the river at this point, especially on the Buckfastleigh side of the bridge, and there are some very fine views of spring flowers on this stretch. The location offers some very good photographic opportunities, and these two pictures, separated by more than 40 years, show the bridge itself from the Buckfastleigh side. The first was taken in the winter of 1968 before train services had restarted, and shows the efforts of the cutting-back gang. The other was taken from a Santa Special on 21 December 2011. The lineside trees have again grown up and been removed, and a home signal – for Bishop's Bridge – has appeared.
Both JB

These three photographs from different eras show the view from the bridge looking back towards Buckfastleigh. The first shows Nos 4561 and 5573 with the 7.48pm empty coaching stock from the annual Buckfastleigh Combined Sunday School excursion to Teignmouth on 24 June 1959. This was the first such train following closure to scheduled passenger services, and was the only occasion when a '4575' Class locomotive appeared on the branch. Their larger tanks put them over the weight limit, and the occurrence was not repeated.

The second photograph, from Dart Valley days, records another double header, this time with Nos 1450 and 1638 on 16 April 1979, an Easter Gala.

Another special working is shown in the third view, with 'Dukedog' No 9017 heading a photographers' special on 4 April 2011 when it visited from the Bluebell Railway. *Peter Gray/Bernard Mills (2)*

The same 'Dukedog'-hauled train is seen again from the other side of the bridge. The second view is from almost the same spot, but with the photographer facing in the opposite direction. This time No 1450, privately owned by Mike Little, heads for Buckfastleigh with the 5.33pm Staverton to Buckfastleigh auto-working on 30 August 2010. Auto-coach No 178, beautifully restored, is also owned by Mike Little, and often appears with the engine. *Both Bernard Mills*

Staverton

Beyond Hood Bridge the line curves gently to head almost due east, running into woodland. The River Dart swings back into close proximity, and the sluices for the mill leat at Staverton station can still be seen here. Although now dry, and long filled in where it runs alongside the passing loop at Bishop's Bridge, the leat is still prominent. On the Totnes side of the sluice stood the old up fixed distant signal for Staverton. In pre-heritage days there was only the level crossing box at Staverton, which was a block post, although trains could not be crossed there.

The first view shows a Dart Valley train from Staverton to Buckfastleigh in April 1975, with the 'Devon Belle' observation car bringing up the rear. It was taken from high up the bank – a very precarious position.

The second picture shows driver Dave Knowling in charge of 2-6-2T No 4555 on an up goods working during the August Gala in 1977, taken from a spot immediately to the left of the 'Devon Belle' observation car in the previous picture.

Finally, a picture taken from the field to the left of the same coach, also in April 1975. Work on lineside cutting back is evidently in progress. *All JB*

Seen from much the same place as the lower left picture on the previous page, 2-6-2T No 5526 heads a single-coach auto-working towards Staverton during a 2010 gala. Since the earlier photos were taken the headshunt from the loop at Bishop's Bridge has been extended back towards Hood Bridge, and coaching stock can be seen stabled on it, behind the train.

In the second view 0-6-0 No 3205 is at the head of an empty stock movement to Bishop's Bridge at a very similar location, and the stock stabled in the headshunt is again evident. This photo was taken from the vantage point of the down Bishop's Bridge starting signal, note the evidence of recent relaying in the form of new ballast, and old wartime concrete sleepers stacked beside the line. *Both Sarah Anne Harvey*

Staverton

The first of these two views of the approaches to Staverton was taken on the opening weekend of Dart Valley services, at Easter 1969, and shows 0-6-0PT No 6412 sandwiched between four autos. Even without leaves, trees obscure the former station master's house and associated occupation crossing, but the road up to Charlie's Cross, above the tallest tree, is clear.

By 1980 it had become possible to run round at Totnes, so trains no longer needed to be auto-worked, or topped and tailed. 0-4-2T No 1450 is in charge of three coaches at the same spot. The loop and its associated signals had been installed several years earlier, but were not brought into use until after the takeover by the South Devon Railway Trust. *Peter Gray/JB*

These photographs were both taken in Dart Valley days, and both also show the site of Staverton loop. The first shows a four-coach auto-train with 0-6-0PT No 6412 in charge at Easter 1969, and it is just possible to make out the Staverton down starting signal. The front of the auto-coach on the left, nearest the camera, is just passing over the crossing by the station master's house.

Although a much more elevated and distant viewpoint, the other photograph shows much the same scene exactly ten years later, this time with 0-4-2T No 1450 and 0-6-0PT No 1638 heading a train back to Buckfastleigh, with loop and signals in place but out of use. *Peter Gray/Bernard Mills*

Staverton

Down on the ground, the Buckfastleigh end of the loop is depicted at different times. In the first view essential maintenance work is in progress on the loop, with fishplate oiling under way in May 1980.

The second picture shows how time and mechanisation move on. Relaying is under way in the spring of 2011, with PW Supervisor Andy Matthews watching ballast being spread by the SDR's road-railer.

The third photograph was taken from a similar viewpoint, but from further back along the headshunt, which is unusually empty – probably because the stock has been pulled out for a 1940s Gala. As part of the event, 2-6-0 No 5322 was hired from the Great Western Society at Didcot, and is here seen double-heading with local resident 0-6-0 No 3205 on a train to Buckfastleigh. *JB/Sarah Anne Harvey (2)*

The first picture was taken from the vantage point of the up bracket signal in May 1980, although despite appearances to the contrary the starting signal next to 0-6-0PT No 1638 was not officially in use. The engine is passing over the occupation crossing, and the station master's house is prominent.

The bracket signal is seen from the crossing as driver Mike Webb eases 'Dukedog' 4-4-0 No 9017 into the loop during the Easter Gala of 2011. The set of points under the locomotive, and the ground signal, give access to the headshunt. *JB/Sarah Anne Harvey*

Staverton

At the other end of Bishop's Bridge loop at Staverton, 0-6-0 No 3205 is on a milk train, setting out for Buckfastleigh – there are tanks behind the coach, which is loaded with churns. Meanwhile 0-4-2T No 1450, no longer a resident of the line and hired in for the occasion, waits in the loop for its next working, which will be to propel its coach the short distance into the platform at Staverton, then continue to Totnes Littlehempston station. *Sarah Anne Harvey*

On 29 May 2011 0-6-0PT No 1639, with driver Giles Gilbert in charge, enters Staverton station with an up brake-van special, having just passed Bishop's Bridge signal box. The South Devon now has four ex-GWR 'Toads' available and, together with a 20-ton BR vehicle and a 'Shark' normally used for ballast ploughing, can assemble a respectable replica of one of these enthusiasts' trains. *Steve Ash*

'Past' photos are hard to come by for this location, since originally there was nothing of interest and poor access. Before the Dart Valley Railway arrived, all that existed was the running line, here shown passing in front of Bishop's Bridge signal box. The wooden first floor of this structure comes from Athelney in Somerset, where it controlled the junction between the new main line and the old route towards Durston. This is the Buckfastleigh side of the box looking towards the station, and the single-line staff for the Totnes to Staverton section is being exchanged for the token onwards to Buckfastleigh. In the fullness of time both sections will become token-worked, once Ashburton Junction signal box is commissioned at Totnes.

The second view also shows a train for Buckfastleigh, with fireman Amanda Hancock about to surrender the staff. The track in the foreground gives access to the down yard at Staverton, wholly installed in heritage days and now used by the SDR's Permanent Way Department.

Finally Bishop's Bridge signal box in seen in the distance in November 2011 as D6737 passes through the station on its way to Totnes with a special train picking up logs; the new yard can be clearly seen. *Richard Bruford/ Sarah Anne Harvey/JB*

Staverton

Staverton station has always had a single platform. In earlier days there were no trees to obscure the view, as seen in the first photograph from across the mill leat, long before it had been blocked up. By this time – probably early 20th century – the station had reached its maximum extent, with both brick stores on the platform in use, together with the cider store beyond the crossing.

The second view shows a typical train of four-wheelers hauled by a '517' Class 0-4-2T engine, and is said to be at Staverton; however, the evident lack of a mill leat suggests otherwise. *Both Totnes Image Bank*

The South Devon Railway Past and Present

This trio of pictures shows the station looking towards Buckfastleigh. The first is the classic 'chocolate box' scene, taken in 1970. Trains are not running, coach No W215W and an unidentified auto-coach are berthed in the platform, and the shutters are still up. There is also the conspicuous absence of Bishop's Bridge box in the distance. The station has its Dart Valley name of 'Staverton Bridge', with the running-in board in the wrong place at the Buckfastleigh end of the platform.

During a frosty January 1979 we have a similar viewpoint, but at ground level.

By 10 March 2011 the running-in board now proclaims 'Staverton' and has moved to its correct position by the loading bay. *All JB*

Staverton

Looking down from the starting signal in April 1980, 0-4-2T No 1450 pauses with a works train, probably having unloaded S&T materials. The down starting signal, seen in the distance, was then controlled by Staverton signal box; contrast this view with the lower one on page 74, when the signal had been transferred to Bishop's Bridge.

The second picture shows visiting 0-4-2T No 1450 and auto-coach arriving at Staverton in August 2010. *JB/Sarah Anne Harvey*

78 The South Devon Railway Past and Present

Staverton's single-storey red-brick station building is reached from the roadside by some steps, flanked by a wooden paling fence. Probably during Edwardian times, wealthy local passengers arrive, their horse waiting patiently while the photographer takes the picture.

In complete contrast in February 2012 we have rather more horsepower, and the wooden hut that was prominent earlier has disappeared. The telegraph pole remains! *Totnes Image Bank/ JB*

In September 1978 Gordon Hall paints the guttering, with bright yellow Dart Valley posters pasted to the walls. *JB*

This wintry scene on the platform at Staverton, looking towards Totnes, is probably during British Railways days. It is obvious that no trains are running, and around a foot of snow has fallen.

Staverton

The 1979 view is also snowy, but there is nothing like as much. Note the different station names and the position of the running-in board. *Totnes Image Bank/JB*

Whether the station staff were ever able to get to the crock of gold whose position is clearly shown in June 1981 is not recorded – perhaps the PW gang was first on the scene. The four-wheel coach W215, known to one and all as 'Liza', was stabled in the bay platform and used as messing accommodation by members of the Staverton Preservation Group. The corresponding present-day view dates from April 2011. *Both JB*

80 The South Devon Railway Past and Present

'Liza' is seen again in the first view, looking from the other direction, while the second view provides the present-day comparison; the barrels remain, but the platform has been tarmacked. The third photograph, dating from September 1993, links with these views, and shows the still-gravelled platform surface and the blue gunpowder van in the bay platform. The interpretation of the GWR colour scheme has changed over the years. *All JB*

Staverton

There are few better places to sit and watch trains than Staverton, which is the quintessential country branch-line station. In early Dart Valley days an auto-train arrives, almost certainly with a '64xx' pannier tank providing the motive power. The old cider store is still in railway hands and is overgrown with ivy.

Some 20 years later 0-6-0PT No 5764 brings a train of maroon stock into the platform on a distinctly showery day – not for nothing is it known as the Wet Country! *Ken Plowman/JB*

The first picture illustrates one of the important uses of Staverton station, for filming for television and cinema, where its timeless atmosphere is much in demand. The particular occasion shown here is an episode of Michael Palin's *Ripping Yarns* in March 1979, which also starred 0-4-2T No 1450. The engine and film crew are seen from the platform between the two store sheds, with the mill building in the background. The very large cypress tree in front of the mill fills much of the background.

The second photograph features the former Exeter Gas Works Peckett, now named *Ashley*, on a rare outing to Totnes in connection with building works at the new station in June 1980. The cypress tree is prominent, as are the single-storey buildings past the mill. Both have now disappeared.

From almost the same position Class 20 No 20118 is seen heading for Totnes on 7 August 2010. When the peak season timetable is in operation, the first Saturday of the month is used to provide a chance for diesels to operate on the branch, although there is always a steam train available for those who prefer them. *All JB*

Staverton

Staverton station is, of course, some distance from Staverton village, but is close to the mill that provided much of its traffic, which in later days came also from the Staverton Joinery. The first view is an Edwardian, or possibly late Victorian, view across the bridge towards the mill and station, with a number of people taking a constitutional.

In the 1979 view some trees have grown, others have gone, but the scene is essentially unchanged. One would probably hesitate to stand around in the middle of the road, though!

By the time the 'present' view was taken, early in 2012, the only significant change was to restrict the width of vehicles able to cross the bridge, with traffic now routed off the A384 via Hood Bridge and Charlie's Cross. *Totnes Image Bank/JB (2)*

84   The South Devon Railway Past and Present

The mill building has been extensively refurbished and converted into luxury apartments, evident in this picture taken from the top of the up starting signal at the station and looking across the bridge.

The width restrictions mean that the few remaining local buses can no longer come across, as seen in the April 1970 view, with Western National service 162 heading for Staverton village. Certain workings were extended to Broadhempston. *Both JB*

Staverton

Up trains leave Staverton for Totnes past the former mill on one side, and the original goods yard on the other. The track and signalling layout today is much changed from the original. These two pictures are taken from the same spot, but more than 30 years apart. The first shows 0-6-0PT No 1638 running into Staverton from Totnes in September 1978; various bits of scrap steam locomotives are in the siding.

In contrast 2-6-2T No 5526 heads for Totnes with an auto-working in February 2012, with the former cider store in the background. This has long been a private dwelling, and now has many solar panels on the roof. *Both JB*

Seen from the up starting signal a '14xx' has charge of five coaches in October 1980, with the 'Devon Belle' on one end and an auto on the other – was there ever a Society for the Prevention of Cruelty to 14xxs? The buildings of Staverton Joinery are prominent.

The second picture shares an elevated viewpoint but is nearer the station, so it shows the cider store rather than the joinery buildings in the summer of 2011. Note that the solar panels have not yet appeared on the roof, and look also at the state of the track (see page 91). *JB/Sarah Anne Harvey*

Staverton

These two views are also from similar viewpoints, this time on the north side of the line. The first shows No 1450 pulling away with a Totnes train, with youthful fireman Chris Woodland; the date is September 1978. The points giving access to the siding are facing for down trains, and are in the distance.

At Easter 2011 'Dukedog' No 9017 is also heading for Totnes, but now the crossover for the siding is near the crossing, and is trailing for trains from Totnes. In fact, the Dart Valley had moved the point towards Totnes, to give maximum length to the siding, but had removed the headshunt, which had been extended by the GWR around 1928. *Both JB*

On 11 October 1958, very near the end of the British Railways passenger service, 0-4-2T No 1427 leaves Staverton for Totnes.

About 12 years later, and now operated by the Dart Valley, 0-6-0PT No 6435 heads a two-coach auto-train for Totnes. The dustcart to the left of the engine is a period piece in itself.
Peter Gray/Ken Plowman

In September 1978 the much smaller No 1450 heads a much larger train away from the station, with one of the bay crossing gates much the worse for wear.

Things are looking much smarter at Easter 2011 when 'Dukedog' No 9017 heads over the crossing; new iron railings and crossing gates greatly improve the appearance. *Both JB*

The token is exchanged, with signalman Cliff Rainbow handing it up to fireman John Kelly on the footplate of newly restored 2-6-2T No 4588 in June 1972.

In February 2012, looking from the same spot, we see the same class of locomotive going in the same direction but facing the other way. No 5526 is on an auto-working, but the token exchange apparatus has gone – it was a Dart Valley artefact – and the wooden palings have turned into iron spear fencing. *Both JB*

Staverton

The first pair of photographs provide a useful view of the old siding connection at Staverton. In October 1980 No 1450 heads for Totnes with its five-coach train, seen from the vantage point of the Staverton down home signal. The ground level photo, from August 1977, shows 0-6-0PT No 1638 shunting the siding, with driver Dave Knowling walking along the track and Gordon Hall looking on.

The down home signal is no longer there, so replicating the shot is tricky. However, the present-day comparison shot from November 2011 is from almost exactly the same location – the old cider store and the station buildings are good fixed points. Note the absence of pointwork, and the state of the track – the area has been completely relaid and reballasted. Matt Tarrant, fully qualified to operate the road-railer seen behind him in the siding, surveys some of his handiwork. *All JB*

Napper's Crossing and Dartington

It is only a short distance from Staverton station to Napper's Crossing – around half a mile. The railway is close to the River Dart for most of the way, and the line crosses a public footpath from the station to the village. Almost immediately it goes over the leat for Staverton Mill by a structure now known as **Southport Leat Bridge**, but which took its original name from the surrounding area known as Southford. 0-6-0PT No 1638 is seen crossing in May 1980 with a train for Totnes, with the railings looking decidedly the worse for wear.

In early 2012 major work was undertaken to arrest the deterioration of the bridge, and to strengthen it where necessary. The track was completely removed and the structure encased in plastic to prevent any pollution of the leat. It was then shot-blasted and painted throughout, followed by replacement of the track just in time to reopen for the February half-term train service, as shown in the third picture. *All JB*

Napper's Crossing and Dartington

Staverton Mill can be seen in the distance in both the 'past' and 'present' photographs, and is fed by the leat that has already passed under the line at Southport Leat Bridge, and does so again next to the crossing here. The River Dart is a very short distance behind the mill, and the whole of the meadow as far as the railway can flood when rainfall is high. Over the years much work has been done on the leat, which now runs between stone walls on the far side of the railway. *Totnes Image Bank/JB*

The original name of this crossing was Staverton Mill Crossing, and despite the public road finishing on the village side of the railway, a crossing-keeper and cottage were required. In some ways this was an easy job, as the train service was never frequent, but the keeper and his family were effectively always on duty. Withdrawal of the Sunday service must have been quite a relief! The 'past' photographs show John James and members of his family around 1880 – he had lost his left leg in a railway accident, and was given this job as a recompense.

The 'present' photo shows that the crossing cottage has been very greatly enlarged over the years. The crossing gates, so long a Board of Trade requirement, have been replaced by an open crossing and a speed limit for trains of 5mph. *Totnes Image Bank/JB*

Napper's Crossing no longer has gates, which were retained throughout Dart Valley days. Mrs Florrie Whitefoot, who lived a short distance away in the centre of Staverton village, acted as crossing-keeper, and was noted for her poetry and her cheerful personality, and for drinking strong tea by the bucketful! Given its use of auto-trains and the proximity of the crossing to the Sea Trout inn and Staverton village, the Dart Valley quickly established a ground-level halt, although there had never been such a facility in Great Western or British Railways days.

In the first photo a '14xx' heads for Totnes in early DVR days, with the down distant signal for Staverton close by.

The halt is seen again in 2011 from almost the same viewpoint – standing on the crossing. *Ken Plowman/JB*

Napper's Crossing and Dartington

Both the 'past' views (right and main picture) are from the early Dart Valley era, around 1970. Both trains appear to be heading for Totnes, and are seen from the track towards the mill, just on the river side of the crossing.

In contrast, 'Dukedog' 4-4-0 No 9017 was pictured at Easter 2011, the viewpoint being slightly altered because of the growth of vegetation. *Peter Gray/JB/Steve Ash*

Napper's Halt can only be used when auto-trains are running, because only those coaches have the retractable steps that are needed to allow alighting and boarding. Don Gibson was a long-standing member of the Dart Valley and South Devon Railway Associations, and died suddenly at Christmas 1996. At Easter 1997 a memorial service was held for him at Staverton church, a short walk from the halt, and a special train was laid on. This consisted of 0-6-0PT No 1369 and a single auto-coach, which was able to use the halt even though the engine was not auto-fitted.

The corresponding photo taken in February 2012 shows that the cutting-back gang has been active, leading to a fine display of snowdrops. The old wooden signal post has been replaced by tubular steel, while the speed restriction board applies to the bridge work at Southford Leat. *Both JB*

Napper's Crossing and Dartington 97

Below Napper's Crossing the railway and River Dart keep close company for much of the way to Totnes. The banks at Dartington have long been a favourite spot for anglers and railway photographers, and these photos and those overleaf were taken from the same place, although looking in slightly different directions. In British Railways days 0-4-2T No 1470 propels its single auto-coach towards Buckfastleigh on 6 April 1957.

The corresponding 'present' photo show 0-4-2T No 1450 propelling its auto-coach towards Totnes in September 2010, with the locomotive unusually facing Ashburton. *Peter Gray/Bernard Mills*

On 3 May 1957, less than a month after the 'past' picture on the previous page, auto-working had finished, and No 1470 is hauling suburban brake W2754W on a similar working.

The same location is seen again on the opening day of Dart Valley services at Easter 1969, with 0-6-0PT No 6412 sandwiched between four autos.

Finally, 2-6-2T No 5526 propels its two auto-coaches towards Buckfastleigh on 6 March 2011. The South Devon regularly provides auto-trains for weekend services between February half-term and the start of daily running at the end of March. *Peter Gray (2)/Bernard Mills*

Totnes Littlehempston (SDR)

The South Devon Railway's site at Littlehempston presents some difficulties in a 'Past and Present' book. When the line was a mere branch of the Great Western or British Railways there was a bit of plain track leading to the junction with the main line. This was on the Newton Abbot side of the River Dart bridge, with the main-line station on the other side. Ashburton Junction once had its own signal box, and the top of this survived as a lamp hut on Totnes station for many years after its functions were superseded by the new box on the up platform.

Essentially, then, there was very little of interest on the site of what later became the station at Littlehempston – the occasional photo of a train approaching the junction, taken from the carriage window, is about it! However, after the Dart Valley took over, trains could no longer run onto the main line, and provision of some sort of terminal facilities became essential. Initially this took the form of a loop immediately on the Totnes side of Hampstead Bridge, which carries a private road over the line about a quarter of a mile from the junction. This allowed locomotives to run round their trains, and ended the practice of either topping-and-tailing longer trains or running auto-services, often with an engine sandwiched between four coaches.

Without a platform passengers could not alight, and construction started at an early stage. The loop was then moved towards the junction, and the platform also had to move. There remained no public access, and plans were drawn up to build a footbridge across the River Dart. These were scrapped when British Rail agreed a running powers agreement for the use of Totnes main-line station, and DVR trains duly used it for four seasons, in 1985-88. After that the costs and operating restrictions became prohibitive, and the footbridge did not open until July 1993, well into South Devon days.

Meanwhile volunteers had been working hard to purchase, dismantle, transport and re-erect the GWR station from Toller, on the Bridport branch. This serves today as Littlehempston station, which also gives access to the Totnes Rare Breeds Farm, and has acquired several other buildings and facilities recovered from different locations, or even built from scratch, together with an enthusiastic team of volunteers.

At Littlehempston station in March 2012, the former Toller building can be glimpsed beyond the large corrugated-iron hut recovered from Bovey Tracey, and now used as a storage space for artefacts and as the station lock-up. *JB*

The South Devon Railway Past and Present

2-6-2T No 4555 makes a fine sight as it heads a Dart Valley train back to Buckfastleigh on 17 August 1975. The first coach is passing under Hampstead Bridge, which carries a private road over the line, so does not allow access to the DVR station site.

The second picture shows the wooden bracket signal being unloaded in 1970 by a gang of volunteers on the same site – it can be seen laid on the bridge abutments in the first photo.

This signal was never erected, let alone brought into use, but a tubular steel post was later placed near the same location, and can clearly be seen in the third photo, taken on 3 March 2012, showing 'Bubblecar' No W55000 forming the 11.30am service from Totnes to Buckfastleigh. *JB collection/JB (2)*

Totnes Littlehempston (SDR)

Hampstead Bridge is seen again from the Totnes side on a very cold day in January 1971. The track on the right is the original running line, and the point and loop were installed by the Dart Valley to allow locomotives to run round.

The second photo was taken from Hampstead Bridge, and shows 2-6-2T No 4555 running round its train in July 1975. The coaches stand on the running line of the original branch, and the loco runs round via the new loop.

The loop here was abandoned when it was moved nearer the junction, so that trains could serve the new platform. On 3 March 2012 the original loop is long gone, replaced by a pile of scrap sleepers. At the time PW work was in progress in the area to reinstate a lead into the bay platform at Totnes, and to bring the new signalling into use. *JB/Alan Taylor/JB*

The steam crane is at work in April 1968, laying panels of track for the first loop; it is viewed across the old railway fence on the same side of the track as the modern platform.

The rather more distant view shows 'Peak' Class 45 No D45 shunting 'Grampus' wagons onto the branch at Totnes, loaded with spent ballast from a relaying job. Hoppers of new ballast stand on the up loop behind this train, on the main line. Earthworks are in progress on the Dart Valley line to widen the formation to allow the loop to be installed, and the fence has been moved to allow this.

The same train is seen again from the new loop, where the track has been laid on what can only be described as a quagmire. The spent ballast was used as a base for this. *All JB*

Totnes Littlehempston (SDR) 103

Appearances can be deceptive: in July 1969, the first season of regular running, newly arrived 4-6-0 No 7827 *Lydham Manor* stands on the running line at Totnes, with the day's service train having approached very close indeed. The latter is formed by a '64xx' tank between four auto-coaches, and at this time should have come only as far as Hampstead Bridge – the loop is not functional.

By March 2012 the cutting sides have grassed over, and much more earth-moving has created the site for Littlehempston station. In both the modern photos landmarks are difficult to pick out, but the viewpoints are much the same as in the late 1960s. *All JB*

Further towards the junction, the Dart Valley's Class 03 0-6-0 diesel shunter No D2192 has ventured to Totnes with a special working in January 1970, with the Hawksworth Brake nearest the engine. Barry Cogar is at the controls, while Brian Cocks stands in the doorway.

A little later in the same year 0-6-0PT No 6412 has also ventured to the site, and stands on the new loop. It has brought materials for the proposed platform, and the sign proclaims that this is the site of the new station. *Both JB*

Totnes Littlehempston (SDR)

By April 1975 thoughts were turning to building a new station. The first picture shows the main-line end of the old loop, with a **DAMO B** van parked in the headshunt.

The other pictures were taken almost exactly ten years later. The first shows Hunslet 0-6-0ST *Barbara* passing the station site with a through working from the main-line station, while work is in progress on the new Littlehempston platform. In fact, this had to be used on Sundays, as trains could not then run onto the main line. The passing loop has been moved along to the new platform, away from Hampstead Bridge, thus giving passengers a slightly longer ride.

The third photograph roughly matches the first, and also shows the new platform, but looking in the opposite direction, with work in progress on the foundations for the Toller building. *All Alan Taylor*

The South Devon Railway Past and Present

The station buildings were constructed by gangs of volunteers, mostly from the DVR Association's London Group, working at weekends and during holidays. The first picture shows the Toller building in situ at its original station in October 1981, with the surrounding area already being taken for new housing. A number of other buildings had already been surveyed, including Heathfield on the former Moretonhampstead branch, but were not suitable or available for whatever reason. The next picture shows work under way to dismantle the structure prior to movement to Devon.

The corresponding photographs show the resited building nearly finished around 1990, and in October 2010. A photo taken at the end of 2011 would have shown it again shrouded in scaffolding, so that repairs could be undertaken at the back. *Alan Taylor/JB/Alan Taylor/JB*

Totnes Littlehempston (SDR)

The branch joins the main line at Ashburton Junction. Strictly speaking, the connection today is with the up refuge, once the up goods loop, although the layout was once much more complex. These two photographs show trains heading in both directions. In the first a branch passenger service waits at the home signal for permission to enter the main-line station, probably just before the line closed to passengers in 1958.

In the second, the Plymouth Railway Circle's final brake-van tour, which had just taken in the Totnes Quay line, heads past the goods shed and onto the branch on 8 September 1962, hauled by 2-6-2T No 4567. *Both Totnes Image Bank*

In a further view of Ashburton Junction, locomotives and coaching stock owned by the Great Western Society are heading to Laira for turning. They had been stored on the Quay line with a view to possible use on the Ashburton branch, but in the event went to Didcot. 4-6-0 No 6998 *Burton Agnes Hall* leads 0-4-2T No 1466.

The other two photographs show the situation at Ashburton Junction today. Taken from the end of the Littlehempston platform, the South Devon headshunt stops just short of the footbridge over the river, with the main line and branch connection in the background. The traditional crossing gate marks the boundary between the South Devon and Network Rail, the track it spans being the original running line of the branch. *All JB*

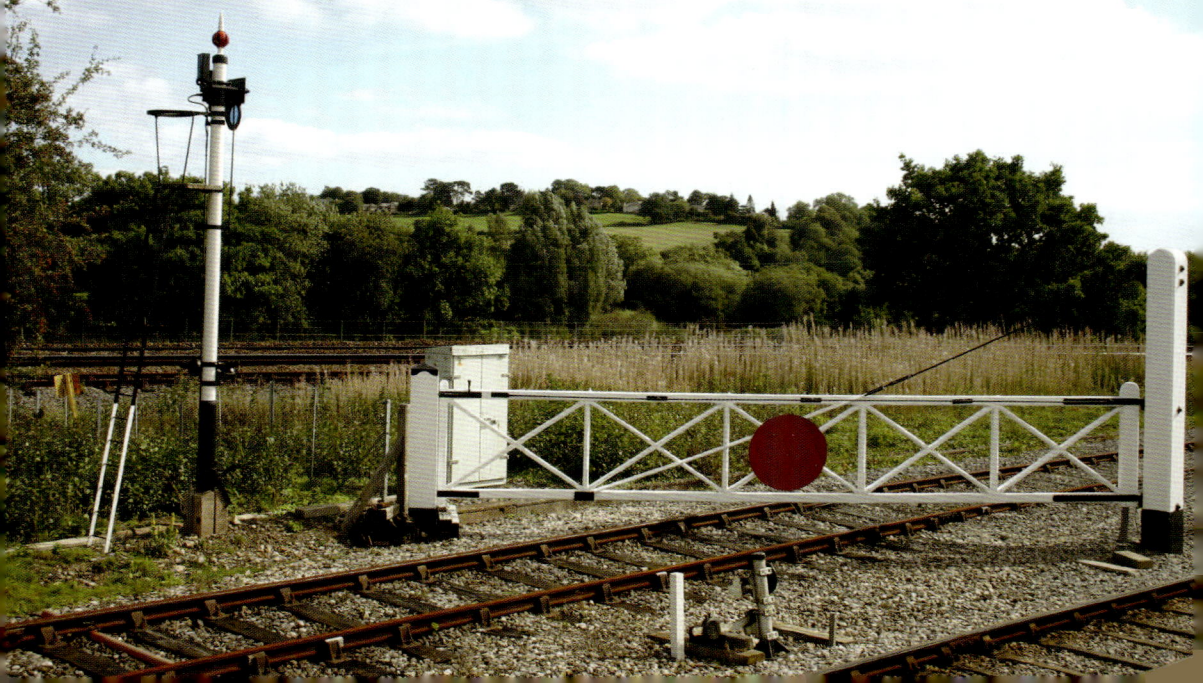

Totnes Littlehempston (SDR)

The top of Ashburton Junction signal box was reused as a lamp hut on the main station after being taken out of use, as seen in the 1970s; it was swept away when the station was remodelled in connection with resignalling in the 1980s.

The second view shows the former lamp hut from Ashburton Junction, which was left in situ for many years and used by PW gangs. Later it was recovered for use on the platform at Littlehempston, where it is pictured in 2010.

The present-day Ashburton Junction box came originally from Cradley Heath, between Birmingham and Stourbridge Junction, and has been re-erected at Littlehempston. During 2012 it was being brought into use to control the station. The Totnes Rare Breeds Farm is in the background. *All JB*

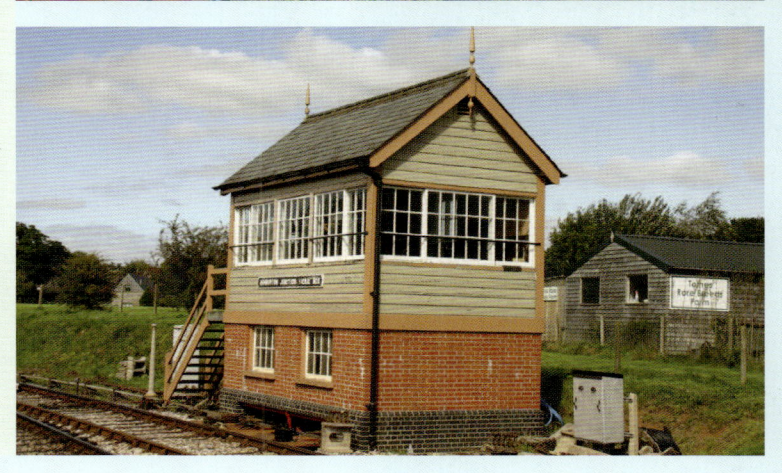

Totnes (GW main line)

Totnes was on the route of the original South Devon Railway main line. Because of the high cost of the atmospheric system most of the line, including this part, was built as a single track, with a timber trestle bridge over the River Dart and the station west of it. The line opened for passengers as far as Totnes on 20 July 1847, and for goods on 6 December. The service was extended from Totnes to Laira Green, Plymouth, on Friday 5 May 1848. The line between Newton and Totnes was laid as broad gauge with bridge rail on longitudinal timbers. The first station at Totnes was similar to the Bristol & Exeter one at Bridgwater.

In 1855 the line became double track all the way from Newton, which involved a new junction for the Torquay line at Aller. Great changes were made at this time to the layout at Totnes station. For many years there were short up and down platforms, with train sheds over the platform lines. A wooden goods shed was located on the down (south) side near the river and junction with the Quay branch. Later, a corrugated-iron garage was provided for the GWR bus.

The station layout was changed again in the 1930s, when Ashburton Junction and Totnes station signal boxes were abolished, and replaced by a new box on the up platform – this is now the Station Café. A serious fire in 1962 saw the goods shed and the main building on the down platform destroyed; the latter was replaced by a temporary structure, which lasted nearly 25 years! Further changes took place in the 1980s when most of the sidings were removed, and the up platform was extended at the Plymouth end.

Totnes station lay between the South Devon's notorious banks. Trains from Newton Abbot first had to climb past Stoneycombe to Dainton Tunnel, then descend the sinuous route towards the River Dart bridge and Totnes. No sooner were they through the station than the ascent of Rattery bank started, followed by Marley

In British Railways days the signalman watches a double-headed express passing through on the down main, while the road through the wooden goods shed is almost clear. The atmospheric pumping house was by then part of the dairy.

Totnes (GW main line)

Tunnels and the descent towards Plymouth via Hemerdon bank. For very many years Totnes had an allocation of banking engines to assist both up and down trains.

The Ashburton branch trailed in on the up side, east of the Dart bridge, with trains crossing over to the down main platform; there was never a separate platform for branch trains. The Quay line junction was on the west side of the bridge, facing for down trains.

The platforms and loops were extended in the 1930s when the signalling was extensively altered. Today rationalisation has greatly simplified the layout, and there is little sign of the complexities of the Quay line, goods shed or milk dock.

From almost the same viewpoint (left), the Ashburton branch train is seen arriving, probably in 1958, in the charge of 0-4-2T No 1470. A lot of people wait on the up platform and footbridge, so there may be a special due, or even a reasonable connecting service.

By 1968 the goods shed had burned down and diesels reigned supreme. The down platform loop has been extended to take in the former goods shed road, while the short siding on the right has been truncated to remove its access to the Quay line, which can still be seen in the background. An unidentified 'Western' diesel-hydraulic hurtles through with lightweight working 1C75.

Finally, in October 2011 a Cross Country 'Voyager' runs in. The footbridge has been replaced, the signal box is a café, and the goods shed is long gone. The platforms have also been extended.
Totnes Image Bank(2)/Bernard Mills/JB

Looking in the up direction, towards Newton Abbot, these views are taken from the footbridge. The first is by far the earliest, and still has some track in the goods shed laid with the baulk road. It is just about possible to make out the bracket signal for the Ashburton branch in the distance. The pointwork in the foreground allows a train to run from the down platform onto the up main line, and thence to the branch, but this route could not be locked or signalled, so branch trains had to shunt across to the up side. This did little for the possibility of providing connecting services, especially as up trains had to run into the down platform, and cross all other lines in so doing.

The second view shows the scene on 25 October 1958, a week before withdrawal of the passenger service to Ashburton. 0-4-2T No 1470 has taken its single coach to the water column, which has replaced the tank, and now runs back into the platform to form a down train to Ashburton. The roads around the creamery have expanded, but otherwise the infrastructure is largely unchanged.

The third picture represents a transitional stage, with the goods shed gone and Quay branch going. The occasion is historic: 2-6-2T No 4555 runs in with empty coaching stock from Buckfastleigh, to form the first train of the last day of services to Ashburton. This worked through to the terminus, and was followed by through specials from Swansea and Paddington.

By May 2011 much has changed. The track layout has been greatly simplified, the goods shed has gone and all the sidings there removed. The signal box is a café, and the creamery has closed. A Cross Country 'Voyager' arrives on a down service, while a First Great Western HST stands in the up platform with a London service. *Totnes Image Bank/Peter Gray/Bernard Mills/JB*

The South Devon Railway Past and Present

Looking in the opposite direction along the down platform, towards Plymouth, the first view is from the ramp. The running-in board advertises 'for Kingsbridge and Salcombe', although both the Ashburton and Kingsbridge branches have closed; however, a bus connection to the latter still calls at the station. A line of milk tanks is visible in the distance, with the concrete water tower just visible behind.

Things have changed today, although the main road bridge has not. The water tank and milk siding have gone, and the up platform has been extended – this was done to accommodate the full length of the original 2+7 HSTs, but today's lengthened sets are again too long for the platforms. Colour-light signals, controlled from Exeter, have replaced the semaphores.

The track machine provides an example of a relatively rare working over the through lines – few trains now pass through Totnes without calling, unlike the old days when stoppers were a relative rarity. *Totnes Image Bank/ Sarah Anne Harvey/JB*

The atmospheric pumping station has long stood watch over the up side at Totnes, and is prominent in the background of the first picture, from the Great Western era. There is just a glimpse of the Italianate chimney behind it, and the station footbridge is covered. The locomotive is 0-4-2T No 1466, one of the '517' Class of tanks, heading a train of four-wheel coaches that were the standard stock on the Ashburton branch at the time. Behind the locomotive is a space where the new signal box appeared in later years.

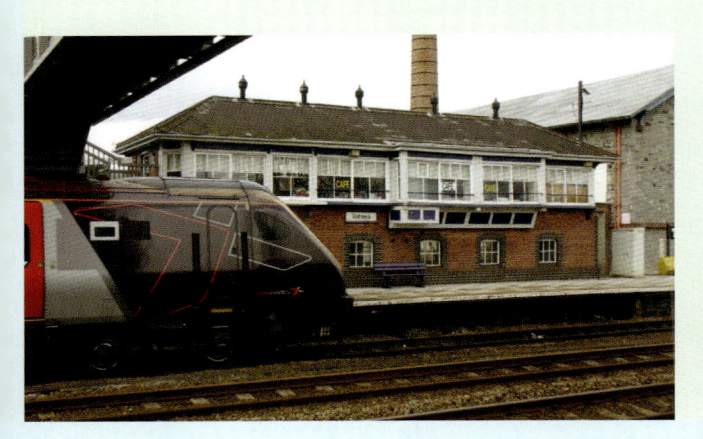

The second picture was taken many years later, in the 1950s, and shows one of the small 'Prairies', 2-6-2T No 4403, in charge of inspection saloon No 800975, standing in the up platform. The pumping station and footbridge are still visible.

In the current scene a Cross Country 'Voyager' arrives. The nameboard, canopy and pumping station are unchanged, and the footbridge is in the same place, although a new structure. *Totnes Image Bank/JB collection/JB*

Looking from the up platform across to the down in GWR days, 0-4-2T No 1163 has arrived with the branch train, formed by auto-trailer No 130.

In the BR era, on 28 March 1952, recently out-shopped No 1470 has arrived with the Ashburton branch train. The canopy retains its full length, and has a station building behind it. A foot crossing is provided for staff to cross the line.

Much has changed in the present-day view, taken in February 2012. The 13.06 Cross Country service to Plymouth has arrived at the station with the usual 'Voyager', in this case No 220004. The awning has been cut back, and the old station building and its temporary replacement have gone and been replaced by the modern version. The rails of the up main line are rusted through lack of use. *Peter Gray (2)/IJB*

Totnes (GW main line)

In the first of these elevated views of the station taken from the footbridge, looking towards Plymouth, 4-6-0 No 1018 *County of Leicester* leads an up express through Totnes in early British Railways days.

The second picture shows the scene in April 1985, during the period when Dart Valley trains operated to and from the main-line station. Modern signalling permits trains to run to and from the up platform, and 0-6-0PT No 1638 is running round its stock prior to departure back to Buckfastleigh.

In contrast, a NENTA excursion from Norwich pauses at the down platform on 23 August 2008, double-headed by a pair of Class 47s. Locomotive-hauled passenger workings are a rarity on the West of England main line these days. *Totnes Image Bank/Alan Tylor/JB*

The two 'past' photos depict the station from the main road bridge, both taken in the era before major rebuilding. The old pumping station and chimney are still in place, together with the train sheds over the platform lines. In both cases a wagon for transporting cylinders of gas stands in the loading dock on the up side. The bright white appearance of the cattle pens on the right is due to the practice of liming them as a disinfectant.

The present-day view still shows the pumping station, but the former creamery chimney is very different. The platforms and loops are much extended, but the goods sidings have gone completely. *Totnes Image Bank (2)/JB*

Totnes (GW main line)

At the approach to the station on the down side there are still signs, but today they are very different. The iron railings are the same, and the house seen behind the 'To The Booking Office' sign is the same as that seen in the modern version. *Totnes Image Bank/JB*

The first view shows the station buildings on the down side before the remodelling between the wars. The goods shed and signal box, still on the down platform, are prominent.

The next pair of pictures show the aftermath of the fire that destroyed the platform building in the 1960s; the temporary replacement lasted for very many years.

Finally, in the 1980s, a modern replacement was built with the aid of funding from Devon County Council. The pumping station roof can be seen on the left, while the remains of the canopy wall are behind the new building on the right. *Totnes Image Bank (3)/IJB*

Totnes (GW main line) 121

The up platform at Totnes was long graced by a fine GWR sign proclaiming 'Totnes Change for Ashburton Branch'. As the first two photos show, it was surrounded by some very fine and carefully tended gardens, for which the station staff – posing for their picture by the nameboard – won awards. There was also a small pond.

Today the only sign is the ubiquitous small name on the nearest lamp post, and the area of the garden has been cut back. The fence has been replaced by a hedge, but the pond remains, together with the screen at the end of the platform canopy.
Totnes Image Bank (3)/JB

Totnes (GW main line)

The approach to the up side has always been dominated by the creamery, first Daws and later United Dairies. In the first photo a stream of lorries has been out collecting churns of milk from local farms, which were then brought in for initial processing and dispatch by rail tanks to London. The up-side station buildings, pumping station and creamery chimney are all prominent.

By 2012 much has changed. The creamery has closed, with milk no longer carried by rail. The larger building on the left of the earlier photograph has been demolished, although the smaller is visible in both. The chimney remains, for the time being. *Totnes Image Bank/JB*

The existing signal box replaced the former one on the down platform, together with that at Ashburton Junction. Charlie Fennamore was a signalman in the old box, and is seen here presiding over his domain, duster in hand. The tops of the levers are brightly burnished, and the floor is spotless.

The box's functions were superseded by Exeter Panel in 1987, and the redundant structure was taken over for use as the station café. However, you can't keep a good man away, and the second picture shows Charlie Fennamore back in his old stamping ground. The café is a highly recommended place to visit while waiting for your train.

The third view shows some of the instruments on the block shelf that allowed the signalman to monitor his signals and communicate with the outside world. The frame was installed at the back of the box, so the signalman had his back to the trains when operating the box. *Totnes Image Bank/ Sarah Anne Harvey/Totnes Image Bank*

Totnes Quay

The Totnes Quay branch was built and owned by the same company as the Ashburton branch, namely the Buckfastleigh, Totnes & South Devon Railway. The company's board took the decision to press ahead after the main branch was finished, and work began in October 1872. It was finished the following September, and opened in November 1873. Despite earlier intentions it was not possible to run directly from Ashburton onto the branch, since it could be accessed only from the goods shed siding, requiring two reversals. This was altered in 1914, when a double junction with both up and down main lines was provided.

The branch more or less followed the mill leat into Totnes, past the livestock market and behind the bacon factory where Morrisons supermarket now stands. It then crossed the mill leat again – just behind where the bus stop towards Paignton now stands – and passed through a crossing gate onto the Plains. There were warehouses there, and the line continued on to the quays themselves, much used for loading timber. Locomotives were not permitted to use the line once past the gate onto the Plains – this was worked by horses.

The crossing onto the Plains, marking the end of locomotive working, is clearly shown by Ye Olde Oake Café. There seemed to be no problem with fixing poster boards to the gates, some carrying bus timetables.

Today's view clearly shows the Royal Seven Stars hotel, to the left of the café, which has long since disappeared, demolished to make way for Coronation Road, which now bypasses much of Station Road. It was in turn bypassed when the Brutus Bridge was built in 1982, allowing the A382 to be diverted away from the town centre. *Totnes Image Bank/Sarah Anne Harvey*

Looking in the other direction, towards the quays, horses once propelled wagons between the quays and the main line. Today the area has been smartened up and trees have been planted.
Totnes Image Bank/Sarah Anne Harvey

Totnes Quay

Another horse-propelled load is being taken for onward shipment by rail, having earlier been landed from a boat. Shop fronts have been added, and today the area is a pleasant one with shops and cafés. Little trace remains of the railway, although the buildings are clearly identifiable. *Totnes Image Bank/JB*

The South Devon Railway Past and Present

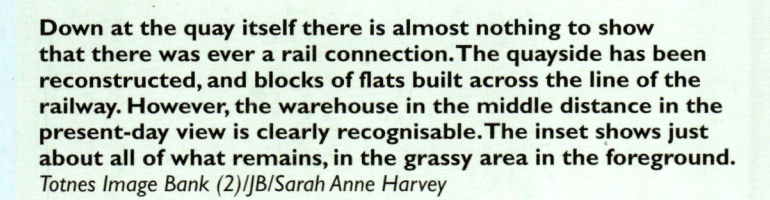

Down at the quay itself there is almost nothing to show that there was ever a rail connection. The quayside has been reconstructed, and blocks of flats built across the line of the railway. However, the warehouse in the middle distance in the present-day view is clearly recognisable. The inset shows just about all of what remains, in the grassy area in the foreground.
Totnes Image Bank (2)/JB/Sarah Anne Harvey